Creative Identity

A Primer on

Who We Are in Who He Is

By Austin Biel

Creative Identity

'A Primer on Who We Are in Who He Is'

By Austin Biel

Creative Identity

Book 1 of the Created to Create Series

© Copyright 2017 Austin Biel

austinbiel.com | catharsisworship.com

Cover design, editing & layout by

Janet (Brandy) Biel and Jazz Biel (rjazzbiel.com)

Other books in the series- Coming soon (titles tentative)

Creative Truth

"Redemption of Artistry"

Creative Strategies

"Blueprint for Artistic Maturity"

Creativity as God's Story

"Restoration of the Kingdom Through Co-Creation"

Fathering Artists: Creative Identity for Pastors

God gave us a vision for a school of worship that would not only raise up a generation of world-changing prophetic warrior-artists, but that would also shift the atmosphere of church government, and provide a place for the creative class to thrive in communion with the Holy Spirit. We are contending for this vision by mentoring and fathering artists, and training them in emotional wholeness, artistic maturity, and a creative drive. For more information, go to

www.catharsisworship.com

Things people are saying about this book:

Austin Biel is one of those rare finds—a master musician who is also a gifted communicator. *Creative Identity* releases insightful keys for discovering a stronger depth of innovative community. The artist will access revelations to expand their creative capacity and productivity. The church leader will find challenging insights that won't read like a protestor shouting outside the gate; Austin writes from the heart of a reformer who loves the church and compassionately points to a more desirable future.

Dan McCollam – Director of Sounds of the Nations and author of God Vibrations, A Song for Seven Mountains, and the Worship Writer's Guide

Pablo Picasso said:

"The artist is a receptacle for emotions that come from all over the place: from the sky, from the earth, from a scrap of paper, from a passing shape, from a spider's web."

This book is a small receptacle of priceless treasures of thought and revelation that is sure to help you identify who you really are as a "creative". Austin's incredible and concise insight reveals the sky, the earth, the scraps of paper, the passing shapes and yes, the spider webs within us all. This is the biggest little book you will ever read.

Ray Hughes, Selah Ministries

Acknowledgements

So many have helped Brandy and me in our journey;
below are the ones who contributed more directly to
this project. But our hearts want to sincerely thank the
MANY dear people that have helped us along our way.
Bless you!

Janet "Brandy" Biel & Jazz Biel edited, typeset and made
the covers. Our younger children, Melody and Tenor
Biel, have been INCREDIBLY supportive throughout our
journey.

Dane-Marc Johnson, you have followed our vision to
the uttermost parts of the earth. Your determination to
stay in relationship has kept us going in darker
moments. We cherish you and celebrate you as our
Jamaican portion of the family!

We wish to acknowledge the support & inspiration of:

Richard & Sylvia Neusch & everyone at True Life Fellowship in Round Rock, TX.

Richard Maisenbacher & Rebecca Maisenbacher & everyone at The Covenant Center in Lakeland, FL.

Ray Hughes & Christ Otto for widening our horizons.

Adrian & Holly Lovegrove for answering EVERY question.

Matt & Bethan Venn for having the SAME vision as ours and inviting us into yours.

Mark, Teri, and Micah Miller for hearing our sound and message, harmonizing with yours, and joining in.

Thank you so much.

In Dedication, from Brandy & Me

To our Father, who has been faithful when we haven't been, who has spoken at just the right time, and who guides us each and every day.

To Richard & Lynn Biel, who have gone above and beyond time and again to support us, and give us grace. Mom and Dad, the years of piano lessons, recitals, prayers and spiritual deposits, have meant more than we can convey. Thank you.

Creative Identity

'Who We Are in Who He Is'

By Austin Biel

Book 1 in the

Created to Create Series

Table of Contents

Foreword

We are living in an age of connectedness undreamt of by previous generations. The internet and other media are connecting more people, faster and cheaper, than ever before. This ought to bring a wider range of creativity and cultures to bear on each other, and yet among many Christians it seem to have the opposite effect. Why create new stuff when we can rely on a handful of talented sources, with their own YouTube channels, to do our creating for us?

Austin Biel writes passionately, Biblically, and from years of experience. He's calling us toward a better understanding of ourselves and our duty to render back to loving creative heavenly Father what He has built into each one. Let's read, enjoy, be challenged, take risks, and fulfill more of our potential for Jesus! Even though most of us won't become famous in this life, we'll have all eternity to compare notes and give God the glory!

Andrew Waugh, Senior Minister, Stockton Baptist Tabernacle, UK

Some Problems...

I've seen some problems. Problems with the world, problems with what SHOULD be the solution, the Church. Problems with people, etc. I'm sure you have too. I've gone as deep as I can to understand the problems. I think I've found a solution, or a part of the solution, that started with revelation and then continued to unfold and prove itself over time in my life. I've gone as deep as I can to understand this solution, and attempt to impart it and enable it.

I submit that Jesus is the answer, that Jesus works through all kinds of things, but most importantly, through the Church. And that when the Church is fully realized and activated, She can heal and change the world.

The problem is simply that the Church as a whole has fundamental flaws that keep her from fulfilling its total purpose. Most people involved in the Church have pure motives, a true heart for God. They have grown up in this flawed system, and thus it is very difficult to accept that perhaps "the Emperor has no clothes". This writing is NOT to condemn the Church, its followers and leaders, NOR is it to bring down faith or try to pull anyone away FROM the Church. But to explore the problems, it is difficult to not appear like someone pointing fingers, making accusations.

If, upon reading this, you start to feel uncomfortable with my characterization of the Church and things surrounding it, PLEASE remember this: – that my heart is to heal, fix, bring truth and love, and ultimately a solution of restoration. You may not agree with my findings or conclusions, but you must receive them from a heart of love and pure motive.

I told my kids that if they came to me just with a problem, that was called whining. But if they came to me with a problem and a possible solution, then that was called working together. I hope to shed light on some issues that are symptoms of a larger disease, and then provide what I believe is a cure toward wholeness. I will also show why I believe prophetically that now is the time for this.

In short, I'm believing for the restoration of the artistic identity to the believer, who then matures both spiritually and artistically. I'm believing for that creative spark to intentionally co-create with the Holy Spirit. When done on a generational scale, we will see a Holy Spirit-led Renaissance that will first transform the Church, and ultimately change the world.

Let me explain...

You are an ARTIST

Say this: "I am an artist. "

> "I was created to create."

Say This. Out Loud. To Yourself:

> I am an artist.
>
> I was created, by the Creator,
>
> to create.

Now, say it again.

> I am an artist.
>
> I was created, by the Creator,
>
> to create.

Many of us live as though we are created to SURVIVE. Survival is important, and we must learn self-defense skills and the ability to provide for our daily needs. Even a drive to accumulate wealth or power can be a mechanism to ensure survival. And yet, our very bodies are designed to decay and eventually die. All of our bodies will die, at some point.

Another variation of this is living as though we are created to CONSUME. It is easy in the modern world to watch movies, buy clothes, and discuss the latest and greatest things, without ever intentionally pursuing the act of creating something of our own.

Yet the act of creation, the practice of creativity, gives us a way to express love, a vehicle through which we can worship. The drive to build and produce, a desire to grow and mature are parts of the artistic identity within us. It is WHY we must survive: to take what is inside of us and bring something out of the depth of ourselves, up to the surface, and out to the world.

I believe that each of us has been given unique skills, talents, and abilities. We are each of us a genius at SOMETHING. We are ALL artists. The purpose of our unique inner skills, talents and capabilities is so that the output of our lives, our ART, is created with our own distinctive Voice.

Do not be distracted by a misunderstanding of this word, "artist". It is, of course, easy to see a painter or a dancer as an "artist" and decide that you are not one. Maybe you have said the phrase "I'm not creative" before, but I hope that you will see that in so doing, you are denying the very purpose of why God created you in the first place. Anything that we do is designed to be done ARTISTICALLY, with creativity and grown into maturity.

A brain surgeon and a naval officer, a priest and a store clerk walk into a bar– oh wait, this is not a bad joke! However, all of these, plus the housewife who is gifted in hospitality, and the gardener who tills the ground, are given gifts and skills. Your gifting may be in building and growing relationships, or it might be compassion and seeing the needs of others. In all things, we were created to create, to live artistically, and to use our Voice intentionally, and purpose ourselves towards maturity.

You are an artist. You were created, by the Creator, to create.

Everyone has a unique Voice; most of us don't use it or grow it. There may be others around us with similar voices, but in our Voice we hear our own influences, our own backgrounds, our own preferences and opinions, etc. Our Voice is the particular way in which we individually express our output.

Your Voice is innate within you, but it must be drawn out, grown, developed; it must be fed. Part of experimentation in our given pursuits is to decide which elements of our experimentation to retain and fold into our Voice, and which elements to consciously edit away from influencing us, even though some things influence us unconsciously.

Pursuing your own Voice and developing it is NOT narcissism; it is not self-centered or arrogant. It is expressing love for our Creator by bringing to the surface what He has placed in us. It is a form of honor and worship to God.

> *"For in Christ lives all the fullness of*
> *God in a human body."*
>
> *Colossians 2:9*

> *"May you experience the love of Christ, though it is too*
> *great to understand fully. Then you will be made*
> *complete with all the fullness of life and power that*
> *comes from God."*
>
> Ephesians 3:19

You were created to bring your own unique Voice to add it to other Voices and give voice to The Voice, HIS VOICE.

In the following chapters, I hope to unpack this in measure – this revelation can and should change the way you live, the way you think, and how you do what you do.

First Mention

Let's go back as far as possible.

In his gospel, John starts off with:

> *"In the beginning was the Word, and the Word was with God, and the Word was God."*

John 1:1

So, this is BEFORE Genesis. God exists. We know about NOTHING else at this point. Everything BESIDES GOD is made of matter, and exists in time and space.

But at this point, none of those things exist.

Then Genesis kicks off the party. God simultaneously creates MATTER, a SPACE for the matter to exist, and binds it to TIME.

> *"In the beginning (time),*
>
> *God created the heavens (space)*
>
> *and the earth (matter)."*

Genesis 1:1

These three things cannot exist without the others, and their creation had to be simultaneous.

This is the first mention of any aspect of God, of His character, of WHO He is. And it happens on the fifth word: "In the beginning, God CREATED...".

So, the most fundamental, foundational aspect we know about God is given the primacy of position in His Word. And that is: GOD IS A CREATOR. First and foremost.

Yes, God is MANY things. But historically, the Church (especially so, since the Enlightenment) has emphasized so many other aspects of His nature and not only de-emphasized His creativity, but especially the creativity He placed within each of us, and the mandate to use it and grow in it.

Ponder this for a moment: consider the totality of everything you know about God, from the Word, your own relationship, and what others have told you. Yes, He is a loving Father and a righteous Judge, a Holy King.

Yes, He is Spirit and became a man. Yes, He is always on time, while existing outside of time.

But the first thing He lets us know about Himself is that HE IS A CREATOR. He has creative capabilities and urges. He is an engineer, a designer, a painter, a biologist and geologist, ALL to serve the purpose of His CREATING.

"This is what the LORD says— your Redeemer and Creator: "I am the LORD, who made all things. I alone stretched out the heavens..."

Isaiah 44:24

"The LORD merely spoke, and the heavens were created. He breathed the word, and all the stars were born."

"For when he spoke, the world began! It appeared at his command."

Psalm 33:6, 9.

To me, the Isaiah Scripture says that EVERYTHING has been made by God, and thus He owns everything. He allows us to use things, to have things, to play and create with things that are ultimately His.

Gifts, talents, abilities – all are His and are from Him. So, when an artist creates, even a piece of art that might be rejected by the Church, or a composition that seems to "defy God," it still gives honor back to the Creator by its very existence.

The creative ability of the artist is God's; thus, unintentional worship takes place every time an artist creates, with or without acknowledging the Creator.

Image

God is fundamentally a creative being, and creativity is important to Him. We have pushed the creative side of God away, and crushed it on the larger scale. I believe that He created man, in part, for creative COLLABORATION.

We humans have free will. We have ideas. And we have the ability to commune with God. These are all things WE/Mankind enjoy that animals, plants, even the angels do not have ! Mankind has a different relationship with God than any other being. We have been given this free will, to have ideas so that we can collaborate with the Creator!

Consider a little later in Genesis, specifically the famous verse:

> *"And God said, Let us make human beings in our image, to be like us..."*

Genesis 1:26

The Message translation says,

> *"Make them reflecting our nature."*

Genesis 1:26

He makes us in His IMAGE? This word is from the Latin *imaginatio*, the same root as imagination, imagery, and imaginary. Consider this: Let us make man with a creative IMAGINATION, LIKE US.

If the nature of God can be defined initially as creative, and then He makes us in His image, reflecting His nature, then it follows that the **FUNDAMENTAL ASPECT OF WHO GOD CREATED US TO BE IS CREATIVE!**

We were created, by the Creator, to create. We were created in His image for IMAGINATION, for IDEATION. Our creativity was designed, in its ultimate iteration, to collaborate, or rather CO-CREATE, with the Holy Spirit.

Genesis reminds us that we all possess the capacity for creativity. Each of us has the ability to imagine, to play with the raw material of our lives, to see things in a new light, and to wrestle with the stuck places within us. As beings made in the image of the Divine Creator, we are given the license and the tools to emulate the creative process illustrated in Gen 1:1; we were Created to Create.

This word 'Artist'

If God is a CREATOR, and He created us in His LIKENESS, then we are designed to be creative beings. If each of us is created by God to be creative, to be capable of creative thought, and each of us has been given gifts and talents from above, then I would assert that God designed us to function in our gifts and talents CREATIVELY.

I would define this word ARTIST as EVERYONE. Webster's technical definition of ARTIST : (noun) One skilled in an art or trade; one who is master or professor of a manual art; a good workman in any trade[1]. Many draw the distinction between folks engaged in the fine arts as "artists", with other activities using other words. Even in the fine arts, "artist" typically means someone engaged in painting, drawing, or other visual art. This is a mistake, and I intend to redefine the word ARTIST in this book. Everyone has been given creative capacity and everyone has been given various gifts.

---

[1] Webster's - Artist

"In His grace, God has given us different gifts for doing certain things well."

Romans 12:6

Later in chapter 12 of Romans, Paul gives several examples of different gifts and abilities, showing that God's gifts to us are of wide variety, and not always obvious to us. I recommend you spend some time studying Romans 12 in the context of what YOUR gifts and talents are.

However, he has given each one of us a special gift through the generosity of Christ. That is why the Scriptures say,

"A spiritual gift is given to each of us so we can help each other."

1 Corinthians 12:7

When God created us with gifts and creative capacity, He made each of us an artist. He gave us the ability to co-create with Him, and to grow into artistic maturity, to each his own measure.

How much has religion tried to tell us that activities related to church life are somehow more spiritual than family life, or work life? That the sphere of the ministry is somehow more important to God than the sphere of business, medicine, or the fine arts? Life is a seamless, integrated, holistic experience, where the sacred is all around us, and if we allow our senses to perceive, it is THROUGH us as well.

Thus, how much MORE spiritual is it to do what He created us to do? Whatever is inside of you, God put there. You were designed and purposed to create with it, to bring good things to the planet with it.

Creativity is like fire – it can be used to destroy or to bring light and warmth. We each have that spark within us, and we are all like construction workers who arrive at a building site. God gives every one of us a different tool box – some may wield the hammer and nails, others a drill or a saw. One may have pipes for water and another wiring for electricity. Each one of us needs to look inside ourselves and find the tools we have been given to co-create with Holy Spirit to help make the world a better place.

Each gifting and area of pursuit has different goals in mind, but each of us use our creativity to accomplish our goals and to grow in our fields. Artistic maturity is something worthy of pursuit for EVERYONE. It is as much a spiritual act and discipline as prayer (an avenue for creativity), worship (another avenue for creativity,) speaking and teaching and evangelism, and so forth. All of those spiritual disciplines use creativity, and I submit that intentionally growing and sowing into your artistic identity is a SPIRITUAL DISCIPLINE. The principles of artistic maturity, which I will talk about later, are for EVERYONE to benefit from, by applying them to their own expression in each of their giftings.

This word 'Anointing'

Let's take a look at the word 'talented' on the way to 'anointing':

All of my life I have been a professional musician, and have spent a large part of my life on the stage. Because my gifts are on display (meaning, they have a higher profile than other gifts), I have been called 'talented' from an early age. While I would receive it as a sincere compliment, it is a bit of a misnomer, and contributes to the very problem this book is trying to solve.

Talent is merely aptitude for a certain area. Some quickly grasp musical things, others relational. Webster's defines "talent" as:

Faculty; natural gift or endowment; a metaphorical application of the word, said to be borrowed from the Scriptural parable of the talents. Matthew 25:24. (and) Eminent abilities; superior genius; as, he is a man of talents[2].

---

[2] Webster's - Talent

My wife is very mechanical and has common sense. Me, I'm not sure how to fix a doorknob, although I think a screwdriver is involved.

But the way we use it, this word 'talent' is misleading. Talent has to do with the innate ability to quickly grasp and apply concepts learned in a given area of gifting. Lack of talent can be overcome with hard work, but the talented one can work much less to acquire skill in the chosen area.

Many people choose to work hard in an area where they aren't talented, and some of those succeed. But EVERYONE HAS TALENT in SOME area. So when we call someone "talented" we rarely have any idea if they have an aptitude for that area or not, but we are seeing a SKILL that is remarkable, which is why they receive a compliment.

Not only has my skill/talent been on display and on stage all of my life, but much of it was in the church, ministering in a church setting. Thus, I "received the accolade of "anointed" most of my life as well.

I would submit a definition of the word "anointing" to be: "God's blessing on man's gifts." Perhaps in some circles this word has come to mean something mystical and difficult to measure in a spiritual sense. Webster's defines anointing as: (noun) the act of smearing with oil; a consecrating[3].

If my definition is true, then it makes sense that many in the Charismatic Christian community will find resonance with someone's art (say, a sermon or a song) and call it "anointed." I don't mean to detract from the spirituality on display in those moments, but their response, in part, is from the creativity and artistic maturity on display, not necessarily "anointing".

When someone functions in their gifting, operates in creativity, and displays artistic maturity, and does so in an overtly spiritual context (like a church service), we can call it "anointed." However, this anointing that is felt can be just as much a soul-ish resonance as a spiritual connection. AND BOTH ARE OKAY!

I try to refrain from describing something as "anointed" or "not anointed", because I am aware of how limitless God is and how finite my perceptions are. To judge the degree of God's blessing on another's output is a chair I am unqualified to sit in. I'm sure that God is moving and doing things that I cannot possibly comprehend.

Perhaps, when a Christian determines something is "not anointed," it is possible that they are actually expressing a PREFERENCE, and dismissing what they don't like or

---

[3] Webster's - Anointing

connect with. The danger lies in dismissing something as non-spiritual when one's ability to discern God in something is so finite.

Using this term, in this way, causes a separation to be made between those who are deemed "anointed" and those who are not. JESUS DOES NOT SEE IT THIS WAY. We are ALL anointed who are followers of God, because we ALL have gifts He gave us, and He has blessed those gifts when we choose to follow Him and express our worship to Him WITH OUR VARIOUS GIFTS.

We can respect and honor one another, and that is good, right, and important. We can even encourage those who have particularly blessed us. But to put an "anointed" label on another person can have the adverse effect of making the labeler assume that they themselves are NOT anointed. This feeds the lie that we are not artists, the lie that we don't, each of us, have something to contribute; and we inadvertently shut down. We allow other lies to keep us from growing, from creating, from RISKING.

Creativity is NOT for the special "anointed" ones. It is for everyone. It is God's gift to us, and we dishonor God and the gift He has put in us not only by saying "I am not creative," but by refusing to acknowledge and use the creativity He has put in us, in our daily lives.

You are anointed. You are talented. You are a certain form of genius. YOU ARE AN ARTIST! Fearlessly walking that out is a big part of why you are here.

Authority

So, mankind is given a creative core, and then authority and dominion over the earth. (Genesis 1:28) And this earth, this reality that we live in, IS A WORK OF ART created by God, down to the smallest atom. And while we are pieces of art, our lives are lived on this canvas called Earth and we co-create with Him into the beauty that He intends.

He gave to us to live in this piece of art, and to be living art inside of it. We have authority to move this art, to interact with it, to change it. Genesis 1:28 gives a vivid picture of God's will for us to use our authority on this earth to make it, reshape it, all to His glory:

"Then God blessed them and said, "Be fruitful and multiply. Fill the earth and govern it. Reign over the fish in the sea, the birds in the sky, and all the animals that scurry along the ground."

Genesis 1:28

I DO believe that we never stop being servants of the most High King, but we don't derive this authority from our place as a servant. When we are young, we have far more restrictions placed on us, as well as more simplistic instructions and warnings. But as we grow and develop, more and more autonomy and freedom are given, and the conversation between God and Man subtly shifts over time from a place of instruction to one of conversation.

Communion is not something servants have with masters. Servants have no authority and no ownership. Their ideas are not needed, not sought, nor are they given place. Servanthood denies the identity of self, abdicating to the Master.

However, we were not designed to live solely as servants, but as Sons and Daughters of the King. Thus we are royalty, we have authority, and we are CREATIVE.

> "I no longer call you slaves, because a master doesn't confide in his slaves. Now you are my friends, since I have told you everything the Father told me."
>
> John 15:15

At this writing, my children are transitioning to adulthood. They have each matured far faster than what I expected and wanted as a father, and I am now having to change the way I interact with them.

Love never changes, but the way it is expressed changes over time as maturity deepens and people change. When they were little children, Brandy and I gave them many "Do's" and "Don'ts". We authoritatively corrected them and gave them instructions to follow when necessary.

But now that they are living adult lives, they are making their own decisions, in small and large things. They are creatively becoming their own persons, owning their own territory, and expressing themselves in their own unique ways.

I don't tell them what to do anymore, but I advise them, based on my heart and what I perceive is theirs. They don't dishonor me, but rather they shape their lives completely informed by my DNA and my heart, yet expressing it in their own unique way with their heart and their DNA..

Now, I would submit that their authority to be their own person comes from me and their mother. We empowered them with identity, based on ours, and nurtured them to be their own someday. Thus, they are all fairly confident in trying new things, forging unique paths in life, and finding their own modes of expression.

Given that lens I see through, I assert that God the Father desires us to GROW UP, take the place of the adult son and daughter, and decide. Decisions are intrinsic to our artistic identity (see the Table of Showbread section, in the "Tabernacle of Moses is an Artist" chapter.) Thus, growing into maturity in our artistic identity is crucial to the overall development of the Christian.

Servanthood to Sonship

Obedience and self-expression are not mutually exclusive. In fact, God is looking for us to mature into the fullness of BOTH.

There is a huge difference between childlike-ness and child-ISH-ness. The first is having innocence and an open mind, having no guile or deceit, trusting and quick to delight. The second is self-centered and demanding, having no empathy or poise, inappropriate, insensitive, and quick to judge, spoiled, as it were.

In the Christian faith, we all start out as children, and without ever losing our child-likeness, we should move towards maturity. We all start as servants, and without ever losing our servant heart, we are designed to grow into Sons and Daughters. (Close examination of the two sides of that coin can yield much understanding.)

In today's typical corporate worship settings, we see a microcosm of the Church as a whole, specifically the aspect that only certain people have the "special thing" and the rest of us are to consume and support them. This exists on two levels: on one level we see the musically talented as designated worship leaders, leaving the rest of us as followers: and on another level, most worship leaders don't even write their own songs but instead predominately use other people's songs .

So, a pitifully few artists create, and are encouraged to write new songs and are handsomely rewarded for it. Then, the rest of us are strongly encouraged to copy them in order to serve the service at a multitude of churches across the globe.

Unfortunately, this breeds a value towards artistic immaturity, and success on the local level is equated with one's skill at imitation, rather than innovation. When the entire culture embraces this, most of us see that we can all worship with modern worship songs, but it is, by and large, artistically stale. We are reaping what has been sown.

Yes, of course, an aspect of good musicianship is a form of servanthood, playing or doing what is asked with a full heart and skill. But MATURE ARTISTRY (something we ALL should aim towards) not only finds a way to fully express one's voice WITHIN the parameters that serve the service, but also grows and develops their Voice, pursuing the fullness of what is in them to be allowed out, and give Voice to their own self, co-creating with the Holy Spirit.

The longer I walk with the Lord, I find His demands on my obedience are higher, while the freedom He offers and His delight at my discoveries increases. I can find my self-expression IN HIM: in obedience to Him is true artistic freedom.

I serve the service all the time; there's nothing wrong with it and much right with it. There are so many pastors who are wonderful and lead great churches. But most pastors would concede that they have been unable to successfully pastor and nurture the creative spark in their congregations, and the artsy creatives in their church have been high-maintenance at best and impossible to deal with at worst.

But now we are moving into a season on the planet where a REVELATION of fathering is coming to the Church. And I would suggest that the very move of God that leaders contend for might lay latent in the creative spark in the people. Co-creating, with intention, with the Holy Spirit, is part of restoring the fullness of the Kingdom on the earth.

And in that fathering wave, the heart and ability to nurture and grow into maturity the artistic identity of the church will begin to blossom and come forth, raising up mature Christians as artists and co-creators, in the Kingdom and for the Kingdom. Until then, we will mostly be fulfilling the directive "Be like this..." - and not really growing.

YOU BE YOU....　　WITH ME　- God

I maintain that a higher level of walking with Him is answering His call: "You be you.... with me." - and growing within it.

God calls us to be creative. He is calling us to be Sons and Daughters, to walk with Him and Co-Create with Him.

Creativity Revealed

What is Creativity?

A few thoughts:

- Creativity is the ability to reveal an aspect of God's character/nature.

- Creativity is what the created do to reveal the Creator.

- Creativity is seed planted within us, designed to be watered, cared for, grown, and allowed to flower and be revealed.

- Creativity reveals both our own personality and the whisper of the Holy Spirit in our spirit.

- The prophet is revealed in each of us through our creative spark, as we learn to hear His voice and interpret it through our Voice.

- God's creation reveals Himself, and reveals US. Our creativity reveals ourselves... and God.

I would point out how each of the bullets above contain the aspect of 'revealing' to creativity. Though we see through a glass darkly... the root of the word 'reveal' is to REMOVE THE VEIL. With the analogy of the veil in place, it implies something treasured, something beautiful, something good has been hidden[4].

God is good, and He created YOU good. Good things are in you, and you are purposed to bring good things to the world. I gently remind you that in this context, the word 'GOOD' is God's version, His definition of good, NOT MAN's judgement of what is qualified.

I say to you, again,　that God made you good, He placed good things in you, and He imbued you with the spark of creativity **SO THAT YOU MAY REVEAL THOSE GOOD THINGS IN YOU.**

BRING IT FORTH!!!

---

[4] Webster's - Reveal

Fear and Identity

Fear is the number one thing that keeps us from walking out our creativity. In the next book "Creative Truth", we will go much more in-depth on fear and dealing with it. But for the moment let me say this:

FEAR EXISTS WHEN SOMEONE DOESN'T KNOW WHO THEY ARE. Fear is ALWAYS a lack of identity problem. When you know who you are, you have no fear.

An example is when a student goes into an audition. A desire to do well, an adrenaline rush because of the importance of this, is natural and normal. The average person is scared and fearful going to an audition. But if their identity in being a student is strong, they will fear less, or none. A student is not expected to blow everyone away with an amazing audition, but rather, a student is expected to audition as part of their learning and growth process. The struggling actress in Hollywood goes on perhaps 5 auditions per week. After an initial season, she starts to understand her identity as a struggling actress and no longer fears any audition.

Or, when one fears a demonic attack or oppression, it usually means that one's authority and identity in Christ has not been solidified. We should not be AFRAID of evil; we should be actively pursuing the REDEMPTION of the earth to expand Daddy's Kingdom, not huddling in fear that we might be tainted in some way.

As young children we are allowed to dance around the room, shout for joy, bang on pots and pans, and color outside the lines. As we grow up, we are disciplined, we are told to sit still, be quiet, and color just inside the lines and no more. Our doodling days are numbered. Our creativity is curbed in favor of a good education and good behavior.

As we discover our design for creativity, we want to stretch our creative wings, but our upbringing hinders us. The fear of going against our upbringing, the fear of not being good enough now, because we weren't good enough back then, hinders us.

And this is the sticking point: Most Christians know WHOSE they are, but not WHO they are: thus the fear. Read that sentence a few more times, please.

Your identity is in Christ Jesus. You are in Him, and He is in you. When Satan questioned Eve in the Garden, asking her about the tree, and why she shouldn't eat of the tree, he, in essence, caused her to question her identity. "God knows that your eyes will be opened as soon as you eat it, and you will be like God, knowing both good and evil." Satan says to Eve that she will be like God if she eats of the fruit, causing her to forget that she is already like God, already created in His image.

This part of the fall, when Adam and Eve lost our identity, has continued throughout history. However, our identity is re-established on the Cross. As Christ dies, His last words, "It Is Finished!" refer to the completion of the full restoration of identity from Adam and Eve, back to their relationship with God in the Garden.

- Restoration of our identity as Sons and Daughters of the Most High God.

- Restoration of our identity as Children of God, and our dominion over the earth.

- Your identity is as a creation of the creator, someone to Co-create with the Creator.

- Your identity is in worshipping Him, and your worship reveals your identity.

- Your identity is in your artistry, and your artistry reveals your identity.

- Your identity is in your creativity, and your creativity reveals your identity.

When you walk in your identity it is a FORM OF WORSHIP to the One who created you! When you intentionally worship Him, intentionally grow and mature, when you intentionally create... **you are being WHO YOU REALLY ARE!**

Two Tabernacles

One can make an intense lifelong study about the Tabernacle of Moses (or Tent of Meeting) and the Tabernacle of David in the Old Testament. If these chapters capture your heart, I urge you to study further than this book (and consult the suggested reading at the back). My attempt here is to explain why I believe, prophetically, that we are living in an age where the artistic identity is being restored across the globe, and to the people of the Lord.

If you don't know the basic layout and furniture of the two Tabernacles, take a few moments and Google it, familiarize yourself with the basic differences and content. Go ahead; I'll wait...

Of course, the Tabernacles are built as a house for God to dwell in. The Ark of the Covenant contains the Mercy Seat, literally the place where God sat. You can't have the Ark without the Tabernacle, and vice-versa. It is the place of God's presence, and the place where man can commune with Him.

There are very striking differences between the two Tabernacles; let me give you a brief picture of my view of the Tabernacle of Moses, and one particular portion that has stood out to me.

Moses was given VERY detailed instructions on how to make the Tabernacle in Exodus Chapters 26-27, and then it was built in Chapters 35-40. This is akin to the beginner in a field of study or a child in the family: they must be given strict instructions, guidelines, and boundaries in the early stages. However, even within the detailed instruction, there was much room for creativity.

God gave the leadership of construction and creation to Bezalel, who is the first mentioned artisan in the Bible, and the only person described as being "filled with the Spirit" in the Old Testament (Exodus 31:1-5). Bezalel thus created the container (Ark of the Covenant) for the glory of God to dwell. The next time in the Bible someone is described as being "filled with the Spirit" is Mary, a person who BECOMES AN ARK to carry and birth the glory that is Jesus (Luke 1:35. See my recommended reading book "Mary" by Christ John Otto[5])

I would point out that this implies that the FIRST MENTION in both Testaments of being "filled with the Spirit" coincides with a mandate to co-create: with

_____

[5] Otto, Christ. Mary

Bezalel to fabricate the Tabernacle, and with Mary to give birth to (co-create) Jesus. So, I submit that being filled with the Spirit comes with an implied mandate to co-create with the Holy Spirit. We are artists! We were created to co-create with the Creator!

Tabernacle of Moses is Artistic Identity

To me, the Tabernacle of David is the truly pertinent and exciting portion, but the following context on the Tabernacle of Moses is necessary. The construction of the Tabernacle of Moses is a study one can go quite deep into. Many interpretations of the symbolism are out there, and I wish to present mine, perhaps a bit simpler than most, blending together three ingredients:

Firstly, the Tabernacle of Moses represents Jesus in micro and macro details. Secondly, it also represents much teaching on worship and an order of worship. Thirdly, in addition, it symbolizes the way we are made, as 3-part beings. In my view, the Tabernacle of Moses represents the restoration of the Artistic Identity back to each of us, and to the Body of Christ. It is the returning of the artistic identity, the capacity of who we CAN be, in our pursuit of Him.

We are actually a spirit, we have a soul/inner man, and live in a body (flesh). Thus, the Outer Court represents our flesh and the beginning of seeking God with praise (Enter His gates with thanksgiving, clapping is flesh striking flesh in the process of preparing oneself to go further, etc.). The Inner Court (or Holy Place) represents our soul/inner man, which additionally has three parts (see below). And of course, the Holy of Holies represents our spirit, and the place where we can directly meet the Holy Spirit.

Please understand I am merely touching on the crests of a few waves here, when the ocean is very deep. I don't wish to rewrite Tabernacle teaching; I'm trying to bring to you what I'm seeing in it, so please forgive me for glossing over what is a VERY deep subject.

Outer Court

The Outer Court, representing our flesh, brings up wounds from the past and present, and sin issues in our life. The artistic identity within us is particularly susceptible to pride-oriented sins, as our decisions yield good things and we forget that He is the good that comes through us. Artistic identity is also particularly susceptible to sexual woundings and dysfunction, as the act of creating and the act of procreating are intrinsically linked spiritually.

Inner Court

Let's zero in on the Inner Court (Holy Place), and specifically its furnishings. The soul/inner man has three portions: Mind, Will and Emotions. Many scholars at this point connect the Lampstand/Menorah to the Mind or the Intellect, and connect the Altar of Incense to the Emotions.

Lampstand

For the artistic identity within us, I submit that the Lampstand, representing our Mind/Intellect, represents the study of our Craft. Meaning, each of us need to regularly and permanently engage in learning and growing in our skill. There are numerous Bible verses extolling the virtue of skill, but many of us get to a certain degree of success, and then fall back on whatever skill we have attained thus far and halt our education. The artist within you should be a lifelong student of the field or fields that are in your heart. He gave us the gift; we return it partly by sowing into the gift.

"Every desirable and beneficial gift comes out of heaven. The gifts are rivers of light cascading down from the Father of Light. There is nothing deceitful in God, nothing two-faced, nothing fickle. He brought us to life using the true Word, showing us off as the crown of all his creatures."

James 1:17-18

Let this be a call to you; to return to your area of endeavor, whether it is cooking, preaching, or basket weaving, and learn! **Those who say that increasing your skill is human-focused are sin-conscious rather than God-conscious.** When you increase your horizons and expand your knowledge, what you are actually doing is sowing back into the very gifts that God gave you!

If you feel a sense of burnout in what you are doing, I would suggest that you haven't been learning anything new in your field, and applying those new things into creative expressions. You have to experience and seek out growth, get inspired and freshen your stagnant inner artist. Another way of saying it is that burnout happens when you aren't learning anything different and you aren't creating anything challenging or unique.

Altar of Incense

For artistic identity, I submit that the Altar of Incense represents our Emotions, represents our passion. Many of those inclined in the fine arts seem to be rather dramatic, up-and-down roller coaster folks. Perhaps they are feeling their passions more deeply than others, However, ALL OF US HAVE PASSION. The key here is to grow into more and more intentional ways of infusing our creativity with our passion, to allow the spark of our passion to become the spark of our creation.

For example, I think that part of the reason Steve Jobs was so successful with the iPhone is not just that it was a better smartphone, but that Steve and the company were so PASSIONATE about every nuance of the product. And people connected with this pursuit and purchased accordingly.

Passion serves numerous purposes for the artist:

. It can be the initial point of inspiration for the idea, project, song, pursuit, etc.

. It can fuel the artist when their strength is flagging, and remind them of the original goal

. It can help the creation resonate with other people, who are affected by or caught up in the artist's passion

The mature artist uses passion as an intentional tool to accomplish their artistic goals

*****Brief side note: One of the Bible's many apparent contradictions I find interesting to include here. Exodus 40:26 and elsewhere states the Altar of Incense is in the Holy Place, but Hebrews 9:3-4 places it in the Holy of Holies with the Ark. One common solution to this contradiction is that in Exodus it is describing the physical location, while Hebrews is showing the theological connection between the Ark and the Altar of Incense. Another is that it is suspected that the Altar of Incense stayed in the Holy Place the majority of the time, but the High Priest took it into the Holy of Holies* *on the Day of Atonement. In my opinion, the incense would have penetrated the veil and the smoke filled both chambers.*

And when the Altar of Incense represents our emotions and the Holy of Holies represents the spirit, it can symbolically imply the strong connection between the things in the spiritual realm and our emotions. Most Christians will admit to a difficulty at times discerning between the voice of the Holy Spirit and the influence of our emotions. I believe they are connected, and as the artistic persona in us matures, we will more accurately discern the difference between our emotions and our spirit.****

Table of Showbread

The furnishing I really want to highlight in this book is the Table. The Table of Showbread is placed on the north side of the Holy Place, or on the right when one enters through the first veil. Interestingly, there is a conflict between translations that either make it of solid gold, or of acacia wood with gold plating. On this table were twelve loaves of bread arranged in two rows.

In my understanding of the Tabernacle of Moses, this would then connect our Will with the Table of Showbread (ToS). And our Will is intrinsic to our artistic identity. Obviously the concept of Free Will is discussed and debated amongst believers. One school of thought says that our purpose on the planet is to be given free will, and then to spend our lives learning to submit that will to God's will.

I would subscribe to this as well, but it is only a piece of the whole. Again, servanthood is always a part of the picture, but Sonship is what we grow into. And in that place, The Table of Showbread represents our own will, our own artistic identity that we must develop into.

We are not robots, awaiting orders from our spiritual master. We are designed to be sons and daughters of the Father, whose heart and purpose for us is to grow, mature, develop, and to create out of the abundance of the gifts and talents He has given. As we mature through life we grow from following our parents' directions, to following their guidance, to making our own decisions. As Christians, we follow the same walk. As young Christians, we begin as servants of Christ and mature into following His ways into sons and daughters, co-creating.

Your will, your capacity to decide, is part of your artistic identity and your identity as a Son and Daughter of God. It is apparent in small things like choosing which color you like for the wall, and in large things like what business deal to make or which college to attend. All of us have already been living artistically from the moment we could make a decision for ourselves!

I would be remiss if I didn't point out herethat this is also where we submit to the earthly authorities over us. One huge aspect of artistic maturity is to learn how to find a way to express oneself fully in any situation, no matter what the boundaries, the canvas, or the tools given. Learning to reside in the Kingdom is to learn how to walk in complete artistic freedom and submission together.

Holy of Holies, Ark of the Covenant

Finally, the Holy of Holies, with the Ark of the Covenant, is representative of our spirits, in communion with the Holy Spirit. As the artistic identity grows in the Lord, this connection becomes tighter and stronger, and the act of creation becomes more and more CO-CREATION. Hearing the voice of the Holy Spirit and intentionally communing is the ultimate aim here.

I find so many Christians who are waiting on the Spirit to speak to them, who use a religious excuse to not grow in their craft, with a false spirituality that "it is all Him". I would say that it is NEVER "all Him". There is always human mixture in the process. Let us not use the Holy Spirit as a pillar we hide behind, a convenient excuse for not moving forward and growing in who we are artistically. God never meant it to be "all Him". He ALWAYS meant it to be "You and Me".

Thus, maturing in your artistry is partly about making more intentional, more mature decisions, and making them an expression of who you are, as you are in Him. The Tabernacle of Moses can give us a picture of the artistic identity in each of us:

- Dealing with the sin issues and brokenness in the Outer Court that are rocks in the flow of our creative stream, and coming into wholeness and holiness

- Submitting our intellect at the Lampstand, making the study of our craft a lifelong dedication

- Intentionally using our passions at the Altar of Incense for greater inspiration and imagination, not being ruled by them

- Yielding our will to His will at the Table of Showbread, and in the process becoming free to be ourselves, in all possible freedom of which humans are capable of.

We are each of us artists, designed to co-create with the Originator. Thus, if all we do is wait on His instruction, if all of our expression is merely to be the tool of what He desires to create, we are not Sons and Daughters, nor are we artists. We become very poor paint brushes, trying to hear His voice and guess at His desires, and NEVER growing into adulthood in our artistry.

I believe that on the planet in this era, the Holy Spirit is restoring in fullness the artistic identity back to the people of God. When you look into the Tabernacle of Moses, you find yourself, your true self, the artistic identity in yourself, because God has placed that portion of his image as Creator there.

A New Order

Through wars and conflicts, the Ark of the Covenant was lost to the Hebrew people for a time. The Tabernacle of Moses at Gibeon continued to operate during this period. When Saul was anointed King of Israel, he wasn't God's chosen one, but rather the people's chosen. Amongst other things, Saul didn't see the importance of the Ark of the Covenant, so even though it was accessible by this time, Saul did not have it brought back to Jerusalem.

So when God's anointed, David, became King, he recognized the importance of the Ark. He orders it brought back to Jerusalem, and after a short detour in the house of Obed-Edom, David brought the Ark back to Jerusalem.

But rather than return the Ark to the Tabernacle of Moses, David instead brought the Ark up to Zion and instituted an entirely new and different Tabernacle. As King, he continued to fund the old Tabernacle of Moses and its operation, but turned his attention to the new Tabernacle of David.

The Tabernacle of David was much simpler than the one from Moses. It basically became one tent that covered the Ark of the Covenant, with the side flaps up so that all could access the Ark equally. Theologically, this is a HUGE development. David funded prophets, scribes, musicians, singers and others to maintain a 24-hour nonstop prayer and worship service, that lasted for 33 years (until David's death).

There are so many parallels and insights to be drawn from the symbolism here. An important aspect is what is written in Amos 9:11 – "In that day will I raise up the tabernacle of David that is fallen, and close up the breaches thereof; and I will raise up its ruins, and I will build it as in the days of old;[6]"

The Tabernacle of Moses was all about atonement for the sin of the people. Now, David's Tabernacle is all about access directly to the presence of God, and Jesus provided us with that access! In the book of Acts, we see the early apostolic leaders arguing over allowing Gentiles into Christianity. James revealed that Amos 9:11 has been fulfilled by Jesus (Acts 15:16), and that we all have the opportunity to be in His presence!

> *"Afterward I will return*
> *and restore the fallen house of David.*

---

[6] Amos 9:11 ASV

> *I will rebuild its ruins*
> *and restore it,"*

Acts 15:16

Many in this time have prophetically been inspired to restore the ORDER OF WORSHIP, in a fulfillment of Amos 9:11. I wholeheartedly agree with this, and have been a part of this movement for a long time with groups like the House of Prayer movement, the Burn, Boiler Rooms and the 24/7 movement. However, I see David's Tabernacle not only as a symbol of the freedom Jesus brings, and not only a prophetically inspired 24-7 restoration of worship, but I see it as a CANVAS, where the artistic identity that is being restored to God's people can grow and mature.

Tabernacle of David is a Canvas

Yes, Amos 9:11 has been gloriously fulfilled by Jesus' sacrifice, allowing each of us access to the Father and His Presence. Yes, we are seeing in this season on the planet a renewed interest and passion for 24/7 worship and prayer in various movements. This 24/7 movement has become a canvas for musicians and worship leaders, creating a space where their own sound can be experimented with, where there are no Sunday morning constraints or onus to contend with.

Honestly, I felt that a much larger variety and maturity in artistic expression should have come out of this recent move. There ARE exceptions, don't get me wrong. I expected to see an artistic renaissance amongst the Christian musicians engaged in the prayer room movement, but instead, we are still seeing little originality. The new sound that has been prophesied for decades has yet to be heard.

I believe this is due not only to the timing of God, but also to a few factors that have kept the development muted, and that this is a prophetic type and shadow of what is taking place throughout the Body of Christ.

As the Canvas of the prophetic Tabernacle of David continues to descend on the planet, many are scared of experimentation, wanting to create a "Presence-driven" atmosphere and sticking with the formulas that have worked in the past. I would submit that His Presence is always among us, simply because He resides IN US and that what is described as His Presence "coming" into a room is actually just our awareness of Him being amplified.

But maturity will refine that sensibility to the point of sensing His Presence at ALL times; that our inner conversation is CONSTANTLY speaking with the Holy Spirit, and that the Bible's exhortation to SING A NEW SONG becomes a passion, perhaps even an obsession.

Let me submit to you that a worship leader is a modern, man-made construct that serves the immature worshipper in corporate settings. Personally, I continue to lead worship in public gatherings all the time. However, I suggest that it is a lower level of service to the people and the meeting, when God is calling us to a higher plane of sonship and daughterhood. In that plane, one doesn't need to give the people familiarity, but one needs to challenge oneself to experiment, to take a risk, to grow and learn. One must answer the call of God to bring all of oneself into the throne room, and with truth and vulnerability, offer up a total and complete sacrifice.

The role of worship leader is prone to create a class of professional ministers; they know exactly what songs, in which order, and what to say to bring about a feeling of corporate worship with the people. They scan the new albums being released, to grab the cream of the crop for use in their services. But that same worship leader is typically not writing, composing, growing in their understanding of God or their craft, and they feel confident and secure because they are so USEFUL to the church.

Though each of these worship leaders has their own sound and they are part of a House of God that has its own unique heart and message, instead of expressing themselves and their own identity they borrow someone else's song/offering and present as their own. They will defend their choice by saying that they are giving the congregation familiar songs so they can sing along.

A value system is in place that says that the congregation participating by singing along and raising hands is what becomes the metric for success in worship. I would state that we are not allowed to judge worship - only God can do that. And thus, what is pleasing to the crowd and to the pastor may not be pleasing to God.

David's Tabernacle is strongly informed by David's background and personality. David developed his identity, his sound, his artistry, and his style of warfare in the fields with the sheep, in solitude. Very few of us engaged in music ministry can say the same. Thus, we typically are given Saul's armor and have no idea who we are, or that it is ill-fitting. All we see is the Sauls in our life smiling at us, and we have no idea how ineffective we are.

In Moses' Tabernacle, the prophetic was kept in check. However, David's Tabernacle system employed numerous prophets, and counted on the ability of musicians and singers to interpret those prophetic words through their voices and instruments. They were trained.

Let us not conflate the building of the church with the advancing of the Kingdom. Providing a congregational worship experience is what most churches feel like they must do. But what I see coming is the average Christian being taught and discipled more about who they are, and their identities as worshippers and as artists. At that point, we will have a canvas that continues to be more and more open, allowing the artist to try new things, develop new sounds, and walk in their own identity as sons and daughters, instead of servants of the current modality.

I believe that the restoration of the Tabernacle of David, in this time, on the planet, is represented by a canvas. And in unpacking this, I believe it represents a call to maturity, an opportunity to grow and develop artistically and spiritually, and a true revelation of what our role here is on the planet. It represents a people tuning into the Voice of God, hearing in the Spirit and then speaking/singing/creating prophetically. It represents a place of health and wholeness, with healing from emotional and spiritual wounds of the past, as well as a revelation of the fullness and the wholeness in which we are designed to operate.

It represents a transition from sin-consciousness to God-consciousness, and a revelation of a God that is a good Father to us, His children, replacing the version of a holy and righteous God that we must be saved from in our sin.

As Ray Hughes points out,

"What David did in the days of the Tabernacle of David was he gave a generation a complete God-consciousness, to the degree that they knew that He would do Who He is and be Who He is in their midst as they praised Him, and [that] He will go anywhere that He's invited and He will stay where He's welcome."

I believe the Tabernacle is a Canvas that represents:

Spiritual and Emotional Wholeness

Artistic Identity and Artistic Expression

Creative Growth and Creative Maturity

After the prophecy in Amos 9:11, you see in verse 13 one of the Bible's verses about creative and restoration and wholeness:

"Behold, the days come, saith Jehovah, that the plowman shall overtake the reaper, and the treader of grapes him that soweth seed; and the mountains shall drop sweet wine, and all the hills shall melt.

"And I will bring back the captivity of my people Israel, and they shall build the waste cities, and inhabit them; and they shall plant vineyards, and drink the wine thereof; they shall also make gardens, and eat the fruit of them.[7]"

Amos 9:13

---

[7] Amos 9:13 ASV

From Childhood to Maturity

Consider a group of children that are put together in a space. Without any instruction or boundary, they will naturally begin to PLAY. They engage their imagination and create characters and improvisation scenes, mud pies and sand castles, crayon drawings and finger paintings. This is a natural, primal instinct that children act on; creation as a normal part of being alive.

We have been given an instinct to thrive, not just survive. Thriving is related to expression, related to growth and learning, related to creating and building. But when we don't know who we are, when our identity is unsure, then we fear, and revert to survival mode.

I believe this fear/survival mode has become prevalent throughout Western culture and pervasive in the Church. This colors all of our decisions, our value systems and our methods. Consider that as soon as our group of children above sit in a classroom, they are immediately surrounded by discipline and structure, told to color inside the lines, sit still, and be quiet, to learn/memorize facts rather than to imagine, dance, and create.

What is absolutely true is that both society and religion avoid raising up the unique artist within everyone. Originality is only called forth by those few who show a certain spark early on. And the rest of humanity, ALL OF WHOM were created to create with whatever talents they have been given, are taught to conform, to copy, to toe the party line and do what is expected of them.

Now, the average person is going to an appropriate school, is studying an appropriate field, and is encouraged to live according to the prevailing "appropriate" norm. Thus, the part of the brain that is creative and intuitive, the genius part that lies within each of us, is turned off, atrophied from disuse, and causes many to proclaim the common curse over their life – "I'm not creative".

At this point I must remind the reader that this God–given artistic identity that each of us has is not restricted to the fine arts, the dancers and singers, etc. This is an identity that has its fruition in EVERY human endeavor, in all manner of gifts and talents, passions and inclinations.

Creativity in preparing a holiday meal, in honoring relationships, in science and math, history and ministry – all can use intentional creativity to further their fields.

What religion and society have done is encourage consumerism as a form of slavery. These concepts have robbed much of the power and potential of the people of God to exert change on their world and to advance the Kingdom.

One development that seems recent (but is actually an ancient situation) is the idea that in ministry, we have sheep and shepherds. We have the 'anointed ones' who minister and the rest of us who don't. We have Christians who shop for a church, making assessments on the quality of the preaching or the worship, and Christian leaders who many times will move in a direction they think people will like rather than what perhaps God wants.

What has been a new development is the scope and far-reaching ability for mega-churches and mega-ministries to be famous, influential, and thus admired or decried depending on your persuasion. As few as 20 years ago, we weren't connected enough to really know who the larger players were. In our current environment of connection, a LOT of comparison between our local churches and these large ministries takes place. A relative handful of churches worldwide are defining things like the latest worship songs, and the 'thing to do' to attract new members or believers, and putting pressure on smaller churches to have similar production values, and other media expressions.

Not only would I submit that not every church needs a TV show, but that those TV shows are almost never doing anything original, merely parroting what the next influential ministry does.

THIS IS PART OF CONSUMERISM IN THE CHURCH.

The consumer is by definition 'shopping' for what pleases them, without realizing that the orientation towards consumerism is SLAVERY. They become addicted to fitting in, spiritual junkies that are looking for their next fix, either the next Sunday or the next CD by their favorite worship leader, or the next conference.

Television shows can become wonderful vehicles for creativity and originality and should exist. However, not every church needs to have one. Whether or not to have one should not be dependent on what the next church is doing but rather on what the heart and purpose of their church is and what God is doing within their church family. The problem is not in the new things we are doing and the new songs we are singing. The problem is that the majority of the church world is in copy/paste mode and not create mode.

I am heavily involved in music in the Body. I think Bethel, Jesus Culture, Hillsong, and recently Elevation largely define the worship songs that are done in churches as of this writing (2017). I get a bit sad that they all have very similar sounds musically, but I have no problem with those churches and worship leaders doing their thing.

The actual problem is that almost every other church in the world is more than satisfied to draw from a very narrow well, to only do the songs from those sources, and worse, to never do original songs from their own worship leaders. The songwriters in the local church could be writing the sound of THAT house, the Word that is spoken to THAT church. The capacity for originality lies in EACH of us. I believe every church could have its own sound, their own songs; uniqueness and maturity is available to ALL.

The artistic identity says that we were not designed to live in survival mode, just trying to make it to the next service or the next mountain top. Artistic identity turns the consumer into a CREATOR, maturely navigating not only the vicissitudes of life but using those things around them as seeds for their own output, their own creativity.

"People tend to believe the conventional wisdom, which is that creativity is somehow an asset that only a few people have. If you're not blessed with this ability, you're expected to become a logical, analytical thinker. When we think we have limitations, that becomes a reality and we begin limiting ourselves."

- Michael Michalko

And thus, we have created and grown up in a culture that, both inside and outside of the Church, puts a low value on average people being original and places a high value on creativity that has a monetary value, while dismissing the rest, thus encouraging each of us to be like batteries for the machine. We are fooling ourselves into believing that our lives are fulfilled by empowering the greater system rather than being individual sources of Divine worship. Each of us creating out of the fullness of who we are, using our own originality and artistry, is worshipping God in our unique ways.

As the artistic identity is restored to the Body of Christ, I believe this will fundamentally change the CULTURE of the Church, and in turn the society around us. You are an artist. You were created to co-create with the Creator. There is a creative identity, an artistic spirit in each of us. The artistic spirit in us is what causes us to ask "why?" rather than just accept what is told to us. It is what causes us to seek out the root of a thing.

The artistic spirit is what inspires us to dig deep, and quest for answers. It is also the part of us that embraces ambiguity and finds beauty in mystery. The artist in us must take what is around us, ingest the culture, assimilate the input into new remixed forms, and then create new culture out of that.

You are an Artist;

what are you going to co-create with your Creator?

Thoughts on Slavery and Freedom

A Consumer sees something for what they can get from it; a Creator sees something for what they can make with it.

SLAVERY	FREEDOM
Consumerism	Creativity
Judgement	Grace
Fear	Identity
Addiction	Connection

We can go on with this chart, but this gives you a brief idea of the discussion here. Consumerism breeds Slavery and creates an Orphaned spirit walking aimlessly. Creativity breeds Ownership and creates a Son/Daughter walking in inheritance.

God's View on Originality

So what is really important, in life or perhaps in your spiritual life? We all know the list of things that guide us forward in our Christian walk, the things we value: prayer, Bible study, and so on. We also see a dichotomy between these and what our culture values. On one hand, stability and solidity seem valuable; maintain a good job, pay your taxes, and so forth. On the other hand, if you have that certain spark, that big idea or that inspired talent, you are rewarded, encouraged to strike out of the box. Innovation means taking a risk, and you should jump off the cliff.

However, the message that is ACTUALLY being sent is one that implies that most people are average and ordinary, and a select few are extraordinary, blessed from birth with that certain "special thing" that separates them from the pack.

Most of the time the "special thing" is originality, and when the rest of us see this, we subconsciously tell ourselves that it must be reserved only for THEM, not for me. Thus, we tend to idolize and place on pedestals those that break out from the pack, and applaud the uniqueness that got them there, while never investing in our own Voice, our own uniqueness.

I believe that God sees this differently. He has placed in everyone a uniqueness, an originality, and I believe that it honors Him and brings Him great joy when we consciously recognize and walk in our own artistry and creativity. And it is for everyone, not just those who we deem as "special".

The heart of a parent is to naturally see their child as special, unique and valued. How much more so is it the heart of Father God to see EACH of His children as special, unique and valued. And yet, when we encounter the face of religion or the view of our society and culture, we are mostly encouraged towards uniformity as a value.

God has placed within each of us unique talents and gifting, personal history, DNA, woundings and triumphs, perspective and personality. Each of us are designed to be unique. In God's eyes, originality for His children is a core value. I propose that sowing into your creativity, maturing in your artistry in whatever gifts you have been given, is not just a nice perk if it is possible, nor is it something only designed for a chosen few.

But intentionally growing in your artistic identity honors God as much and possibly more than the rest of the things we do to intentionally honor Him. Spiritual growth/discipleship always has a list of the things we should do to grow as Christians, and I humbly submit to you that creative growth and development should be on that list, for every believer.

The Bible is full of encouragements towards originality, the easiest of which are the admonitions to "sing a new song", and yet songwriting skill doesn't seem as directly spiritual as feeding the hungry or going on missions. This is part of the lie of what culture and religion deems as valuable, versus how God views originality.

You are designed to be a culture-shifter, a culture-creator. In order to affect change in a culture, you must inhabit a place so intensively that you can be responsible for it, respond to it, contend for it daringly, to CULTIVATE it. Thus, WHERE you place yourself is hugely important. You may find that you are engaged in a culture that is not in your heart to change.

Lance Wallnau says "Take what bothers you most as an invitation to join God in solving that problem. Seriously, it just might be that you are anointed to solve a problem and that problem is the thing that bothers you." I would add that this implies that if you are entirely satisfied with the place you find yourself, you might just be in a swamp of stagnation.

You are an artist. You were created to co-create with Holy Spirit... WITH YOUR LIFE. This is as much a part of your identity in Christ as any other part, and one that many of us, maybe most of us are not walking in with intentionality.

I encourage you to move towards MATURITY, both spiritually and artistically. And a huge part of getting there is pursuing WHOLENESS, both emotionally and spiritually.

The next step after discovering your artistic identity is to rewrite the lies you have been fed with the truth and imprint it on your heart, to guide your decisions and point of view. Book 2 in this series, "Creative Truth", will break down many of those negative concepts that hold you back, and help get you moving towards wholeness and maturity.

Further Reading

"Seeing Christ in the Tabernacle" by Ervin Hershberger, 2007 Vision Publishers

"The Tabernacle of Moses: The Riches of Redemption's Story as Revealed in the Tabernacle" 1975, by Kevin Conner

"The Tabernacle of David: The Presence of God as Experienced in the Tabernacle" 1995, by Kevin Conner

"Bezalel" by Christ John Otto, Belonging House, http://www.belonginghouse.org/bezalel/

"Mary" by Christ John Otto, Belonging House, http://www.belonginghouse.org/mary/

"The Artisan Soul", by Erwin McManus, HarperOne, 2014. http://erwinmcmanus.com/

"Imagine: A Vision for Christians in the Arts", by Steve Turner, Downers Grove: InterVarsity Press, 2001

Works Cited

1. Webster, Noah. Artist. Webster's 1828 American Dictionary of the English Language. (2010). The Editorium; Compact ed. edition

2. Webster, Noah. Talent. Webster's 1828 American Dictionary of the English Language. (2010). The Editorium; Compact ed. edition

3. Webster, Noah. Anointing. Webster's 1828 American Dictionary of the English Language. (2010). The Editorium; Compact ed. edition

4. Webster, Noah. Reveal. Webster's 1828 American Dictionary of the English Language. (2010). The Editorium; Compact ed. edition

5. Otto, Christ, Mary (2016). Belonging House Creative.

6. Amos 9:11 (ASV) - In that day will I. Retrieved from https://www.blueletterbible.org/asv/amo/9/11/s_888011

7. Amos 9:13 (ASV) - Behold the days come saith. Retrieved from https://www.blueletterbible.org/asv/amo/9/13/s_888013

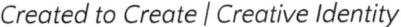

www.ingramcontent.com/pod-product-compliance
Lightning Source LLC
Chambersburg PA
CBHW071245170526
45165CB00003B/1239